The Biggest Little Fan of the Red Ball Express

A true Christmas fable

by Jay Michael Jones

Vabella Publishing
P.O. Box 1052
Carrollton, Georgia 30112
www.vabella.com

Photos courtesy of the Daily Oklahoman

13-digit ISBN 978-1-938230-23-3

Library of Congress Control Number 2012923055

10 9 8 7 6 5 4 3 2 1

Dedicated to my sister

"If a picture paints a thousand words, then the joy and wonder on little Lela's face is worth nothing less."

-   Lon Chaney, Jr. /
    Hollywood, CA

Six children peered down the long train track behind their house. It was early summer but already the sun was merciless in the sky, smothering Elgin, Oklahoma in a scorching blanket of light. The twelve-year-old boy shaded his eyes with his hand against the sun and said, "It'll come any minute now."

"I don't see why we have to wait for it, it's just a train and it comes by all the time," his sister Ginny complained as she picked the goat's-head stickers off her socks.

"But it's fun," Lela protested beside her. "Mama said the train men travel all the time and they probably get really lonely."

"I wouldn't get lonely, I'd just get me another job," Buddy declared, and Ginny rolled her eyes at both younger sisters.

"Buddy, you be able to stay out of the corner at school, much less get a job! And Lela, if you want to wave at these old noisy things all day long then go ahead. I'll wave some but I don't plan to make it my goal in life. I want to do something."

"We can go play mumbledy-peg," eleven-year-old Annie said in reference to their favorite pocketknife game. "Papa let me borrow his old penknife."

"Yeah, let's do that!" Six-year-old Buddy quit chewing on her braids and kicking in boredom at dirt clods.

"You better not cut yourself again; Mama had a fit the last time you played."

"It was an accident, I done told you that." She and Annie quarreled all the way back to the house, where a pair of trees offered weak shade from the bright Oklahoma sun.

The boy picked up the baby of the family and put him on his shoulders. "You coming, Lela?" he asked as he and Ginny turned toward the house.

"No, I want to stay and wait for the train."

Before he could reply, they heard the train whistle blow far down the track. "Suds, we might as well stay and wave," he told Ginny.

"Domio!" squalled the toddler on his shoulders. "Domio, go!"

"Don't pull his ears, Bird," Ginny said with a laugh as she pulled the baby's hands away from their oldest brother's vulnerable ears. "You're gonna make Domio look like Dumbo!"

"That's all I need," Domio groaned.

The thundering roar of the approaching train made their stomachs flutter with anticipation and the whistle gave them all a tingling feeling up and down the spine with each blast. In the hot flat sandy land of southwestern Oklahoma the sound of a train whistle meant movement, excitement, travel – wonderfully foreign things to the children. As the train sped toward them along the tracks Annie and Buddy rejoined their siblings and the six children waved as a team. The train crew in the engine cab waved back. The children continued to wave at the strangers in the passenger cars and did not stop until the brakeman in the caboose returned their wave.

"Well," Ginny said grimly as it went out of sight, "There's another train full of people going somewhere I ain't."

"Yeah, because other ten-year-olds go all over the world on their own," Domio grunted. "Let's go on home, Papa will be here soon."

"First dibs on mumbledy-peg!" Annie declared.

"Second!" Buddy yelped.

"Bud, you better go get something on your arms so you won't poke your elbow with the point this time." Buddy scampered off to follow Domio's practical advice.

Lela watched the train leave until she could no longer see it. She skipped after her brother and sisters with a smile on her face. She liked waving at the train people and decided not to miss a single day from then on.

Twelve-year-old Joe Junior was better known as Domio ever since a sister could not get an immediate handle on the name "Joe". He was a lanky boy with curly red hair and did not complain when asked to take on the responsibility of looking out after his sisters, even though he would have rather goof around with his friends.

Annie was eleven and quiet like her brother, painfully shy and willing to stay in his shadow. Her short black hair was curly like Mama's and her button nose was like Papa's. Annie was an artistic child who illustrated the little 'family newspaper' she and Domio made for their own amusement out of the white meat wrapping paper from the butcher.

Ginny Lou was a ten-year-old spitfire with long black braids, angular features and high cheekbones beneath big brown eyes. She was the natural-born leader of the Watson children, athletic and bold. Ginny was a beauty even in her youth with a quick, volatile temper and a skewering wit.

To the family and the world at large, six-year-old Mary was known as Buddy after a character in her favorite book. Uncles and aunts sometimes forgot what her real name even was. The teachers at school chafed at the nickname, and Buddy chafed at the name Mary. Buddy's complexion was pale and her baby blonde hair was beginning to darken to brown. She was painfully thin but that did not mean she was weak. It was Buddy who decided she wanted bangs, and when Mama was not looking Buddy sawed off a handful of her forelocks with a pair of safety scissors from her school box. Mama managed to correct the haphazard attempt, and the bangs curled wildly across her daughter's forehead. The safety scissors were immediately confiscated since heaven only knew if Buddy might decide to fashion herself a crew cut.

The baby of the family was almost two years old and even thinner than Buddy. Aunt Helen worried that she would not live to see two, because "that child eats like a bird." The name Bird stuck, although over the course of time she garnered many nicknames in an effort to dispel the first name that seemed longer than she was tall. She had curly chestnut hair and sleepy eyes. As the baby Bird was petted and pampered by sisters and occasionally overlooked by Papa Joe, who gave up the dream of a basketball team full of sons.

Lela Rae was seven and brown as a potato. Her round face held the bright smile of an eternal optimist, and her long thick braids hung like church bell ropes down past her shoulders. A middle child, she lacked Ginny and Buddy's tempestuous natures and their penchant for tomboy behavior. Lela went out of her way to please her parents not to curry favor, but because she sincerely wanted to give back.

This generosity extended to others. Early in the summer of 1955, seven-year-old Lela began to steadfastly wave at the passenger train that ran twice a day on the track past the field in the back of the house. The sight of so many people on their way to somewhere far away captivated her imagination, but she especially liked to see the train crew. The passengers might never be the same, but the same men waved back at her from the mighty locomotive. The train raced by on its daily run from St. Louis to Fort Worth and back, and she never missed a single day. Under the crushing weight of the summer sun's heat, Lela was ready in the field at four o'clock.

The crew was impressed by her loyalty. People always waved to passing trains as if it was an unwritten law of the land. But engineers Harry and Malvin with Dutch the brakeman noticed every day whether rain or shine, the same little girl waved in the same field. "She never misses," they said to each other with a smile. It was not only the regularity that impressed them: despite the oppressive heat of the dry dusty flat land, her enthusiasm did not wane. She leaped and waved with the same amount of gleeful abandon as when they first noticed her.

Many times there were other children with her and the crew guessed most of them were siblings. But no matter who might or might not be present, the crew looked forward to the sight of the leaping little girl with the cheerful greeting and flying black braids. Occasionally they threw apples or wrapped candy to children along their route so they made certain to have something on hand when the train rolled through that particular dusty little town. In the summer of 1959, Malvin tired of referring to her simply as "the girl with the braids", so they threw her a note tied to a stone to ask something about her.

"They wrote me, look! They want to know about me!" Lela squealed in delight as she held the note in a tight grip.

"Well, that's pretty nifty," Ginny had to admit.

"They don't have very good aim!" Buddy declared. "They missed her!"

"You are a fink," Lela grumbled. She went into the house and wrote a carefully penciled note on a clean sheet of a Big Chief tablet: *I am Lela Rae Watson and I am seven years old. I am a good girl in the second grade. I made all A's and B's. I hope you are fine. I hope you write back.*

She took her letter to the train station in town, where the stationmaster promised he would see that it got to the afternoon crew. She continued to wave every day at the train from the center of the field behind the row of shabby little houses along the tracks.

Joe Watson Senior was an oil field roustabout, a dirty and sometimes dangerous job in the endlessly rolling wheat fields and cattle pastureland of southwestern Oklahoma. He was a barrel-chested Creek Indian who was one-quarter white, and he lamented the recessive gene that gave him a balding pate with a monk's-ring of dark red hair. His wife Georgia was quarter-blood Creek Indian and talented in the necessity of stretching a dollar as far as possible. She was a tall, angular woman with curly jet-black hair whose rapid production of children neither slowed her step nor altered her patient demeanor.

All that summer the Watson children found ways to amuse themselves until school started again and they would have something to occupy their quick and curious minds. Joe and Annie worked on their 'family newspaper', and Ginny and Lela and Buddy played with plastic toy horses under the trees in the back yard. They busily smoothed out little roads with the fleshy side of their hands and used sticks and scraps to create pastures and barns. There was no television set in the house so they read every book brought in as soon as it appeared. Domio hung around with friends down the street but the Watson girls had no patience with them. The boys could not play mumbledy-peg nearly as well and were considered pathetic in the eyes of the Watson crowd of the tomboys. Ginny could not abide the lack of talent.

When it was time to return to school in the fall, Lela was concerned for the crew of the Red Ball Express. "I might not make it home to see them, Mama. I have to wave to them or they will think I don't like them any more." Mama was sympathetic but she would not agree to ask the school to let Lela out early in order to wave at the train. "Then Bird will have to wave for me, if I don't make it home in time," Lela decided. "Will you watch the clock for me, and send her out in time to wave?"

"Of course I will," Mama replied with a smile.

Lela had Bird practice every day all the week before school started so the baby would know what to do. Bird mimicked her big sister leap for leap and wave for wave. By the time Sunday afternoon came Bird ran out the back door at the sound of the faraway whistle, Lela was satisfied that her stand-in was ready for action.

On the first day of school Lela's leg danced nervously as she sat at her desk, poised for flight as soon as the bell rang. As soon as it sounded she darted out the door and ran as hard as she could toward home. Her feet pounded hard on the dirt road as her legs pumped like pistons but despite her best efforts, the train was already out of sight by the time she pushed open the back gate and ran into the field. Bird still stood in the middle of the field, waving at the disappearing train far on down the track.

"I missed it!" Lela wailed. "I missed it!" She was inconsolable all evening, and declined the jump rope contest Ginny thought up to distract her. Paper dolls were no good and plastic toy horses held no charm. Even

Papa's wild storytelling could not keep a smile on Lela's face for long. Finally he sat her down on his lap.

"Now Lela Rae, you can't always get what you want. I know you want to wave at the train and that's nice, but you have to go to school. There's just no way around it. All you kids are smart and Mama and I want you to go to college someday. I went for a while, and I want you to go when it's your time. To do that, you have to go to school every day that you can. Now, Mama said Bird waved just like you taught her and did a good job. You can wave at the train in the morning and just leave it up to her in the afternoon. The trainmen understand. They know all little girls your age have to be in school," he said firmly but kindly. Lela nodded.

"I almost made it in time today," she ventured. "Can I at least try to make it?"

"Sure you can," he said with relief as he hugged her. Later to Mama, he muttered, "And here I thought Buddy and Ginny were the stubborn ones."

"They're all stubborn," Mama said mildly. "They are Watsons, after all." Papa regarded her with an upraised eyebrow, and Mama could not hold back a smile. Papa laughed.

Lela was not the only disappointed one that day. The train crew was surprised to see only the baby waving wildly in the field. "Well, I guess the little pig-tailed girl just gave up. It's probably too much for a little girl in school and all," Harry the engineer remarked with dismay. His partner Malvin pursed his lips but said nothing.

Papa came in from work that day without whistling "Sweet Georgia Brown" as he usually did. He was quieter than usual and stared blankly at the dinner table as Mama placed the large pot of hot pinto beans in the center of the table along with the freshly made cornbread. "Joe—" she began.

"I got laid off today, Georgia," Papa said softly.

"Me 'n Craig laid down for our naps today," Buddy chirped, "but we didn't nap." Buddy's stories about her adventures with her best friend Craig usually captured Papa's attention immediately. The story topics ranged from School Paste is Tasty but We Aren't Supposed to Eat it Like We Did, to I Can Cut Craig's Hair Easier Than

Mine. These stories invariably concluded with a round of schoolroom corner-standing for the irrepressible pair of first-graders. Buddy was so brashly pleased with her ability to confound her grumpy teacher at every turn that neither parent could dampen her enthusiasm. Both Papa and Mama tried to be angry but Buddy saw the way Papa's eyes twinkled whenever he said, "you're a chip off the old block."

This time she and the other children sensed that something was not right that night; Papa looked pale despite his perpetual tan, and the sudden look of concern on Mama's face was frightening.

"Oh, Joe," Mama said with a sigh. She quickly ladled beans onto the children's plates in an effort to distract her curious brood.

"I guess we're going to have to get used to a lot of beans," Papa sighed. He liberally covered his own beans with black pepper and hot homemade chow-chow. The children breathed a little easier at this familiar scene, but the normally boisterous din was muted.

"What is it, Papa?" Domio asked. Papa glanced at his son and saw strength in the boy's gaze, and it steeled his own resolve.

"Well, the folks at the oil company decided I worked so hard, they're going to give me some time off to be with my family," he said lightly. Buddy and Lela cheered at what they thought was good news; Domio, Annie and Ginny glanced at each other knowingly. They knew what "laid off" meant, because some of their schoolmates' parents used the same phrase for what meant a calamity for a large family. "Don't worry," Papa reassured them. "There's always work for a man who wants to work. I didn't just spring up from an oil field, you know. I was a carpenter before I worked in the oil field. I did other things before the war, too. I'll scare up something." The confidence in his voice was so firm, the older three children relaxed and smiled again.

As Papa and Mama readied for bed that night, Mama quietly voiced her concerns. "Joe, we're already scrimping to make ends meet. Are you sure you can find something?"

"Sweet Georgia Brown, I'm certain of it," he said with a cocky air as he took a sip from a bottle he had taken from his jacket pocket. She glanced at it, and frowned. He saw that frown. "Now, Mama, don't worry. There's work out there."

"Enough to celebrate early?" she asked a tad sharp.

"It's called a pre-emptive strike; we had them all the time in the war."

"That's not all you had in the war," Mama recalled. "You also had M.P.'s who knew you by your first name." Papa looked a little disgruntled but he put the bottle away.

Every day after school Lela ran home as if chased by a wild thing, and every day when she reached the gate, she could see the caboose disappear out of her line of sight. But she continued to run, and saw a little more of the caboose each time. On Saturdays and Sundays she waved extra hard. The train crew on duty those days waved and smiled at the familiar sight.

On the third week in September as the train approached the house Malvin let out a howl of delight and nudged Harry. "Look at that!" Bird was in the middle of the field in her assigned place to wave but over to the side of the yard, racing so fast to join her that the black braids flew straight out behind her back, was Lela. Her excitement to make it in time to meet the train was tempered only because she was out of breath. Still, she jumped and waved the best she could.

"So that's where she's been. She's been trying to make it home I guess after school!" Harry said.

"Sort of renews your faith in humanity, doesn't it?" Malvin asked with a grin. Harry nodded in abject contrition, but his partner added softly, "I knew she wouldn't give up on us."

Mama was hard-pressed to stretch their remaining dollars as the days passed. Papa went to the labor pool every day at first, but as one day dragged on to the next his confidence waned. Many men were laid off by the downturn in the oil business and what few jobs were out there had been snapped up quickly. Papa's earlier stint as a carpenter did not help obtain much work, either. When he finally did get a job at a construction site, he heard from his friend Carl that Mr. Kelly the foreman was not honest.

"I've heard some tales about him and none of them are good," Carl explained. "He's just fishy, that's all."

"I've got to do something, Carl. We can't live on fried egg sandwiches, and the chickens are eating more corn than they're worth. Besides, I've got a Union card from my old outfit in Muskogee. If my hammer's not good enough, I'll try to work in the office. I was an accountant when I was younger. This old dog's no threat to some young pup."

"Yeah, but just watch out. Kelly might boast a good game but his handshake doesn't have much integrity."

One day Papa took a board from a stack of lumber and paused as he held it. A large knot was in the plank. Papa knew from experience that a knotted board spelled trouble for a construction crew, since the hard knot could bend or break off nails. He showed the board to a co-worker, who told him to set the board aside and get a good one. Bad boards sometimes slipped in by mistake.

Later that afternoon he found a few more knotted boards, and he wondered who could have missed so many.

The next day as he got his lunch box from the officer trailer, Papa noticed an invoice on a desk. Curious, he looked it over. The secretary picked the paper up and Papa gave her a friendly grin. She smiled back.

"This is a big project. Mr. Pierce is spending an awful lot of money on it," he said casually.

"Yes, it's big all right. He's planning to put another like it in Ardmore."

"That invoice there," Papa said with a nod at the paper in her hand – "is that the price for that stack of wood out there, or for the whole job?"

"No, it's just for the one that was delivered yesterday."

"That doesn't seem right."

The secretary glanced it over and saw nothing wrong. "Oh?"

"That's a lot to pay for scrap lumber."

"Oh, you're mistaken, Mr. Watson. We only buy quality material for Mr. Pierce's projects."

"Uh huh," Papa said evenly. She did not look him in the eye. He shrugged and took his lunchbox outside.

Later that week, Papa looked over the board pile with concern as he ran his fingers over a large knot in a plank. Other boards with knots might be useful since the knots could be simply cut away and the knotted piece left unused, but there were far too many in the pile. Papa put down his hammer and took the board to the construction trailer. Mr. Pierce was not in, but Mr. Kelly was and he was not pleased to see Papa and the board.

"This lumber you're using is inferior grade. You're going to have a mess on your hands trying to work around all this knotty pine. I just thought you ought to send it back to the lumber yard and get some better quality wood," Papa explained.

"Okay, so? It's no skin off your teeth," Mr. Kelly replied. "It can't all be knotted."

"Don't get me wrong. Some of it is okay but what isn't knotted, is bent and twisted. I saw the invoice when the load arrives. You're just throwing away good money on bad product."

"Watson, I'm the supervisor for this site. There's nothing wrong with that lumber as far as I can see. Don't worry about it." He leaned on his knuckles and added with emphasis, "Get it?"

The secretary stood behind Mr. Kelly, and she frowned. She caught Papa's eyes and gave a small shake of her head.

"Oh," Papa said sarcastically, "I get it, all right."

Mr. Kelly drew himself up straight. "We probably have more men on site than we need, now that I think about it. Now if you're not happy here, we can fix that."

Papa realized what he meant, and thought about how long it took him to get the job. "I haven't said I was unhappy. Look, I need the work."

"Well, the last thing I need is some journeyman telling me how to do my job. This company does all right by me."

"I'm sure it does. And what Mr. Pierce doesn't know won't hurt him or you, will it?"

"Don't be a sap. Mr. Pierce just looks at the bottom line and he's never cared to know how it gets that way."

"I don't believe it!" Papa declared.

"He didn't get where he is today by being a Boy Scout. Besides, who's he going to believe, a faithful longtime foreman or a drifting oil field rat?"

The insult burned, but Papa wasn't licked yet. "If it wasn't for the downturn in the oilfields, you jaspers would be begging for help!"

"Of course a smart old guy like you has all the answers," Mr. Kelly said as he picked up a cup of coffee and took a sip. "There's bound to be some place that can appreciate that sort of thing. I'm sure you can find plenty of odd job roofs to patch up on your own, to support your kids!"

"Is that so?" Papa roared, his temper finally getting the best of him. "Well let me tell you, you cheating little cockroach, you can take your crew and shove it!"

He pulled his hat firmly down on his head and marched out of the office. He clocked out and walked home. Perhaps it was better if he simply quit work rather than allow Mr. Kelly to drum up a false reason to fire him. Papa doubted if "Being Too Honest" was a reason Mr. Kelly would tell the unemployment office.

"You did what?" Mama exclaimed in alarm at his story when he came in that afternoon. He slumped down further into the armchair in the front room. She handed him a cup of coffee before she turned back to folding the freshly taken-in laundry from the line in the back yard. Bird sat in the floor and turned the pages of a worn Golden Book and told herself the story in her impossible-to-interpret chatter.

"I told him to go shove his precious job list up his —"

"Joe!" Mama said as she jerked her head in Bird's direction.

"—nose," Papa finished with the air of an unjustly accused man. Mama gave him the wry grin of a woman who knew better. Papa clarified. "He was one of them cocky little jaspers who knows which string to pull. He's set all nice and neat in an office job, and he knows which book he's cooking. Easy for him to say no! I got suspicious when all that bad material kept showing up at every delivery."

"Can't you talk to the boss?"

"It won't do any good. Kelly will poison my name before I can open my mouth – if Mr. Pierce really is honest. A lot of dishonest men put on nice congenial airs to look good. Shoot, they might even find a way to blame me if something happens."

"Oh for heaven's sake," Mama groaned.

"George," Papa sighed, slumping further in his chair, "I know it wasn't a smart thing to do walking out like that but if you work for a crook, you'll be a crook yourself. I just couldn't do that."

"No, it's best that you don't," Mama agreed. She offered him a smile.

Off in the distance, the whistle of the four o'clock train sounded faintly. Bird jumped to her feet and trotted importantly out the back door. Papa also rose and together he and Mama followed the child. They stopped at the back door, but Bird was already heading for the middle of the field. She planted her legs firmly and began to wave as soon as the train came into sight. Lela skidded into place just as the train reached its zenith for the pair, and they propelled their arms gladly as Harry and Malvin waved from the engine cab. The children continued to wave until they made certain Dutch the brakeman in his usual place on the caboose got his fair share of the waving.

Papa sighed. "Well, at least our kids are keeping up with their jobs," he said.

The five a.m. train crew would not make their usual round one October morning, and Malvin and Harry took the run for them. It promised to be a rainy, miserable day. While they were not particularly enthusiastic about the day they did not mind doing the favor. They bundled up for the cold ride.

Lela happened to awaken early when she heard Domio leave to deliver his newspapers. She got up at the smell of coffee Mama had on the stove for Papa. She smiled shyly in the doorway, and Mama waved her in and gave her a little coffee in a cup to enjoy. As she sat at the table and sniffed at the aromatic steam with delight, Lela heard the distant wail down the track.

"Mama, it's the train! Can I go out and wave, can I please?" she pleaded. Mama glanced her way and saw the hopeful seven-year-old already had her rain slicker at the ready. During school days Lela was not usually allowed to get up for the five o'clock train, but since she was already up Mama saw no harm in it.

"Well... put on some galoshes and I imagine you can," Mama replied. Lela rushed to comply, and streaked out into the field where she waved with both arms. The light from the open kitchen door flooded a rectangle into the field so Lela could see her way to and from the house.

"Well, I'll be – I want you to look at that right there!" Malvin exclaimed to Harry as he pointed out the window. "Now that's what I call dedication!"

"She's waving at us, she's waving at us! I don't believe it; five o'clock on a rainy morning!" Harry whooped. He pulled on the whistle and waved back at her. "That little Lela Rae is a marvel!"

That night they told their families what had transpired. Malvin's wife enjoyed the sparkle in her husband's eyes as he described the scene along the tracks.

"Well, her dedication is certainly above and beyond the average train-waver. I wonder about her, Mal. What do you suppose she'd like for Christmas? Maybe you could toss out a little toy or some candy on Christmas day." The next day, the crew tossed a weighted note into the field for Lela.

"Dear Lela, What would you like for Christmas?" Lela read breathlessly.

"What do they want to know that for?" Buddy wondered as she peered at the note from over Lela's shoulder.

"They're just making conversation," Ginny told Buddy. "A lot they care about a bunch of kids like us. Come on, let's go play." Ginny and Buddy went out to tire swing, so Lela got out her Big Chief tablet and sat at the table.

Lela wanted a baby doll more than anything in the world, a doll she could love and take for walks. She wanted lots of clothes for her doll too, and these things she wrote in her reply. More notes were exchanged back and forth as the trainmen asked about the rest of her family and what they might want. Domio wanted board games, she reported; Annie wanted drawing paper or books. Ginny wanted a hula-hoop, and Buddy wanted a stick horse. Bird wanted – well, Bird was just a baby but she was sure to want a toy for Christmas.

By the time she finished this correspondence, Mama assigned everyone a task to set the table and they followed her instructions as they sniffed the air.

"Beans again, and Spanish rice," Ginny said as she set out the dishes.

"Mama, I am not going back to school again," Buddy announced firmly and she placed the cloth napkins at each plate. "That ol' music teacher just don't like me because she talked to my first grade teacher, the one who told me I shouldn't read. Well I could; so what? Mama, what's wrong with it?"

"Nothing is wrong with it, Buddy. I guess the teachers just aren't used to having children who can read as well as you do."

"But they don't get mad at Ginny an' 'nem!"

Mama put the bowl of Spanish rice on the table and turned a patient but firm gaze on her second youngest child. "Buddy, it's not just the reading. It's the paste-eating and the scissorwork and the blackboard eraser fights between you and Craig, and Lord knows what else you cook up. Now I want you to stop riling your teachers. You know how to behave, and I for one am getting mighty tired of hearing from *them* about *you*." The tone in Mama's voice was as stern as the children had ever heard from their soft-spoken mother, and Buddy quickly ducked her head in submission.

"Okay. I'll be good." Mama heard the reluctant tone in the word 'good' and wondered if that meant good for a month, a week, or a few days. She decided to let it go. Buddy was contrite enough, and Mama secretly enjoyed hearing the bedevilment her daughter caused. The condescension in the teacher's voice as she scolded about Buddy did not sit well with Mama. As if poverty could not buy manners! Manners had nothing to do with Buddy.

She might be a little pampered by her namesake aunt but mostly, Buddy was born with a stubborn streak a mile wide. Mama preferred to curb her daughters, not break their spirits. Life would do that all too soon if things did not improve.

"Look here; Lela wants a Tiny Tears doll," Malvin read to the others in the switchyard.

"Well, what the hell is that?" Dutch asked.

"It's what she wants," Malvin replied. "And she's gonna get it!"

"Why, these are things any kid wants," Harry noted as he looked over the list. "And it's nothing we can't find, y'all. Nothing fancy, just toys and stuff."

Malvin brought the letter home that night to show to his wife Eva. "It's from that little girl who waves. It's just a little wish list, nothing special or outrageous."

"But it should be special; it should be a fairytale for her!" Eva exclaimed when she finished reading. "Mal,

I'm going to go get that doll tomorrow and I'm going to make some extra sets of clothes for it. I have plenty of fabric scraps around here."

"Well, doesn't it come with clothes already?"

Eva gave Malvin a look that said *Oh you men!* "Yes but little girls love to change their babies and dress their babies, and fuss over them and feed them."

"All right, I sure won't complain if it means more for Lela. And don't bother with scraps; get some fresh new cloth at the store and sew your little heart out!"

"I'll make a pinafore and a nightie and a pretty little dress with puffy sleeves – oh, this will be fun!" Eva's heart was already set on a full trousseau and Malvin was happy to encourage her on it.

Papa could not find work anywhere, no matter how hard he tried and how willing he was to do the least thing. No sooner did he hear about work than someone quicker beat him to it. The family was now on welfare, which burned Papa's pride but provided almost enough money to pay the rent and what utilities they had. Still, food was problematic and Christmas presents were out of the question.

"I'm off to find work up in the northeastern part of the state. I'll stay with Big Mama while I hunt around for a job. Now don't you kids look all so unhappy! I'll only be gone until New Year's, and I'll see Uncle Tommy too; he lives up there. I'll get me a job quick as that and we'll all be fat for Christmas." The children's faces all brightened at the mention of Uncle Tom, their favorite of Papa's relatives.

"Gee, I want to go too," Ginny said.

"You kids stay here and keep out of mischief," Papa said with a smile.

"I ain't done nothin'!" Buddy objected.

"Yet," Papa rejoined, and they laughed together. "And you better not do anything or I'll get my fly-back paddle after you." Buddy straightened quickly and nodded. "Now Domio, you are the man of the family until I get back. I want you to take care of your mama and your sisters. Okay?"

"Okay." There was not a lot of choice for the twelve-year-old, but then he did not consider that there was any other choice. Papa went north to hunt for a job.

Malvin contacted Mama one afternoon while the children were in school. From the cab of the train the scenery just flashed by like a dream, but up close he found a grim reality. The house was a drafty row house, its clapboard sides weathered gray and the window screens were brittle and brown. Sparse grass was scattered throughout the dirt yard. The bicycle leaning against the porch had no rubber tires, only steel rims. It also had no seat, but there was a canvas bag the newspaper office supplied for every deliverer dangling from the handlebars. The rider had to remain standing on the pedals constantly while moving. Malvin shuddered out of sympathy for its rider as he knocked on the door.

The interior of the house was neat if sparsely furnished, and Mama's demeanor was so regal it might as well have been a palace. She ushered him inside and offered him a cup of coffee. He thanked her and got down to business.

"M'am, as I said I'm one of the engineers on the Red Ball Express. Your little girl Lela has come to mean a lot to us trainmen – she's sort of our mascot, you see. She gets out there and jumps and waves and oh, it just warms our hearts. We see a lot of people waving but we've never seen anybody as consistent as her."

"She loves to wave at you, she really enjoys it. I hope there will be a track near where my husband is looking for work up in the northeast of the state. She wouldn't be happy if not waving at a train."

Malvin felt a pinch of dread inside. "Oh. Well, I hope so too. There's a lot of folks out of work, all right.

Um, if you don't mind my asking, what are your plans for Christmas?"

"I just don't know what I'll do about Christmas," Mama said helplessly. "My son does as best he can, but he's only twelve and he's only got a job delivering newspapers. He's big for his age but I want him to stay in school. He was put ahead a year in grade – they wanted to put him up two grades – and I just can't let him drop out."

The trainman was alarmed. The idea that a bright twelve-year-old boy might have to drop out of school for the sake of what little money a bone-rattling bike ride could bring in nagged at Malvin. "No, you can't let that happen. Mrs. Watson, we'd like to sort of give back to Lela what she's given to all of us – all your children, of course. I hope things will get better for you all but just in case, we'd like to help make your Christmas for you somehow."

"That...that would be wonderful," Mama said, her queenly head still high but the tears of gratitude gathered on her lower lashes.

At that moment, Bird toddled in with a Golden Book under her arm, talking in her baby language. Nonplussed at the strange man seated on the couch sipping coffee, Bird crawled up to sit beside the man and began to "read" aloud, tracing the lines of text with a skinny little finger.

"Can...can she read?" Malvin asked in astonishment.

"No, Bird is only two. That's still just a little too early even for my brood," Mama said with quiet pride. "Sssh, Bird; we have company." Bird pointed to a picture in the book. Her eyes squinted shut as she threw her head back against the couch cushions and laughed uproariously. Then just as suddenly she straightened back up and resumed talking her way through the text. "Guess it was a good part," Mama said, calm about the abrupt reaction.

Malvin was startled for only a moment, and then smiled. *I suppose you have to have a good sense of humor around here*, he thought.

Papa wrote home as often as the stamps and envelopes he brought with him lasted. He stayed at his mother's house and hit the sidewalk every day in search of employment. Life at Big Mama's house was no picnic. She was a stern, frosty Creek Indian widow who criticized his every move. Papa's brother Tom worked on the Turnpike, and that was the first place Papa applied but they would not hire him. Place after place turned him down, and it looked to be a repeat of Elgin's job market.

"I don't see how your wife puts up with you. You drink too much and you don't deserve her," Big Mama said in her flat Indian's tone of voice.

"I know," Papa mumbled as he turned over his boot to inspect the sole. It was worn through at the ball of the foot. He got day work every now and then. When he could he sent money home. He thought he was doing pretty well to send Mama ten dollars; it was ten dollars more than he had to send her the week before.

Big Mama sniffed and said it was a pittance for a woman with six children. "I raised six of you, and I know it takes more than that."

Papa scowled. Santana Watson had been a rancher when Oklahoma was still Indian Territory. He died of cancer at far too young an age, and Papa had idolized him. Once the Depression hit, Big Mama could not run the ranch well enough to make a living, so she sold it and moved to town near her eldest daughter. In Big Mama's eyes, Papa was too much like Santana – charming, flirtatious and weak. Santana's weakness was an appreciative eye for the ladies. Papa's weakness was whiskey.

Papa's best pair of pants now had a hole in the seat. "The labor office takes one look at my worn suit pants and hands the only available job to some younger rascal in better clothes," he wrote to Mama. "I'm nearly fifty years old and if clothes really do make the man, my pants are telling a poor story on me." One day he was able to get a temporary roofing job, and with the windfall he bought a new pair of work boots. "I stand a better chance of getting a lasting job if I have decent shoes on my feet," he explained in a letter home. "I knew you would understand, but it is good to read it for myself that you do." He lived for the arrival of her letters. In his, he did not mention Big Mama's opinions; if he found a job steady enough to bring the family north to join him, he did not want to make his wife dread the move. Either Big

Mama might turn against Mama, or she might eventually turn Mama against him. He continued his job search and helped Tom make repairs on Big Mama's house. It was "the least he could do", Papa was told.

"I guess if I just went out and hung myself, Big Mama would say it was the waste of a perfectly good piece of rope," Papa said to Tom as they nailed down shingles.

"And a perfectly good tree," Tom agreed. "Don't pay her no mind, Joe. She's never been a lightheart, you know. I don't know how –" Tom bit off his words and did not finish his sentence but Papa could guess what they would have been.

I don't know how Daddy ever put up with her. It was not something a man should say of his own mother, and Santana would have been the first to correct them.

The story of the loyal little girl with the big heart was widely known to all the workers up and down the Frisco line, so other train crews added to the Christmas collection the Red Ball Express crew started. Someone came up with the catchphrase, "Railroader's hearts are as warm as firebins," which caught many a rail man's fancy. At first the donations were only collected from the rail workers up and down the lines, but eventually even the main office in Saint Louis was petitioned for a donation. Few among the rank and file thought the matter would even be considered but it would not hurt to ask to loosen a few corporate purse strings in the spirit of giving.

"Wouldn't that just be the thing for that little girl to see her own train wave at her for a change?" the crewmen asked one another. The idea took hold, so the Red Ball Express crew put in a bold request for an even more special Christmas for Frisco Railroad's biggest little fan.

Frisco's Superintendent of Railroads called Malvin and Harry into his office in mid-November. They did not have time to change from their uniforms. They stood uneasily in the office before his desk. "I understand you want to stop an express train on a holiday."

"Yes, sir; that is what we'd like to do," Harry said as he uneasily toyed with the railroad cap in his hands. He had just commented to Malvin a few days earlier that the worst they could do is say no. Now he wondered if maybe the worst was yet to come and it just might come to him and Mal. "It would just be for a little while, so Santa Claus could deliver a few things to her and her family."

"Do you have any idea just how much it would cost the company to stop a passenger train on an express route?" Malvin and Harry glanced at each other in consternation. "More money than you will ever make in your lifetime, I'll tell you that right now," the super answered himself. Dutch eased into the room along with some of the other crewmembers of the Red Ball Express.

"It, it won't be for very long, and it's for a good reason," Harry stumbled over his words.

"I believe I'd like to hear this 'reason'," the super drawled. Harry turned to Malvin with a look that indicated Harry was fresh out of worthy inspiration.

"It's like this," Malvin said as he adjusted the wire frame glasses higher up on his thin nose. "Every train that ever ran a track gets lots of folks waving at it, but this little girl is different. She's out there waving every day she can; you can see her bustin' her tail running to make it home from school in time. She even tries to get up at five in the morning to meet the morning train, a little girl up at *five in the morning!* Summer, winter, spring, fall; morning, noon, evening – it doesn't matter to her, she's out there waving. We've been writing notes back and forth with her. She's a smart little thing and makes good marks in school and is just the sweetest thing you ever saw.

"But her family has fallen on hard times; I mean *hard* times. Her daddy hasn't worked a real job in months and he's still out beating the bushes to get one. They have six kids, all of them smart as a whip and good as gold from what I hear tell, but there's hardly enough money for their mama to be able to feed them all. It just isn't right that this sweet little girl's family has to go without. Their welfare check doesn't cover near enough. They don't ask for much from anyone and they have even less. Lela – that's her name – she never had to wave at us but she does it because she wants to. If you only knew how much it means to us to see her out there every day to wave at us, to make us feel like we count, to let us know she cares, it..." It was not about them, and Malvin shifted the emphasis back where it belonged. "Well, it breaks my heart to think that she's going to wake up Christmas morning after being so good and after all the joy she's brought to us, and find out Santa flew by her house faster than the Frisco Railroad."

The other crewmembers murmured in agreement, and Harry nudged Malvin with his elbow in approval of his eloquence, and nodded. "That's right, partner."

"Well my Lord, Mal," the superintendent said as he stretched in his chair, "I guess I'll just have to go with you when you stop there on Christmas and meet this little wonder."

"*When* we stop? You mean we can stop?"

"From what I've heard these past few weeks, we can't *not* stop," the superintendent explained with the grin of a man who has pulled a fast one. The crew elbowed one and another and punched Dutch in the arm in silent celebration.

"Ow; that's my *arm*."

The superintendent continued, "The boys in the head office like that 'railroad hearts are warm as firebins' thing you boys have been using, and the publicity sure won't hurt the railroad. We'll get the newspapers to cover it. With all these interstate roads being built, Frisco needs all the good will it can muster."

Mama was told the train crew had something special in mind for Lela and the children and that she should have them up and ready for the early train on Christmas morning. By Christmas Eve, Domio had gone out and chopped down a scraggly little pine tree from a nearby pasture for them to decorate.

"That's a nice tree, Joe," Mama said later. He was almost too tall to kiss on top of his head anymore.

"Thanks. Um, what will you do about...?" He glanced at the stockings and then back at her.

"It will be all right," she reassured him. "Go on to bed."

Domio did as he was told, squeezing into the girls' bedroom. He could not sleep on the couch as he usually did, since it was Christmas Eve. Papa and Mama always claimed Santa would not come if children were up and awake, so Domio had to make a pallet on the floor and sleep there.

"How do you suppose Santa travels all over the world in one night? Can reindeers really fly that fast?" Lela wondered as she tucked the covers around her and Buddy.

"If reindeer fly at all, then I suppose traveling fast is easy enough for them," Annie pointed out from her spot on the lower bunk.

Above her Ginny said, "I left some carrots on the porch for the reindeer. Boy, are we ready for him this year!"

Domio frowned. "That's wasteful!"

"Mama said it was all right, I asked first! She said it was thoughtful. Reindeer have to eat. Santa's fat enough."

"Well, okay," Domio decided, "if Mama said it was okay."

"Whose boss are you?" Ginny demanded.

"Papa said to take care of everyone, and I am going to do it," Domio pointed out.

Lela sighed. "I wish Papa could be here for Christmas. It doesn't seem right without him."

Buddy suddenly sat up in bed. "Would you guys be quiet! Santa won't come if we're still awake!"

Ginny teased, "Santa's going to bring you and Craig Hill big ol' pots of school paste!"

"Is not!"

"Is too!"

Domio sharply order, "Ssh! Go to sleep!" The girls quieted down. Domio tucked his nose under his blanket to get it warm as he grumbled, "Gee, it's stuff like this that makes me glad I sleep on the couch."

The five children dropped off to sleep one by one.

They were up long before time but Mama made them wait in the bedroom until daybreak. She led them out to the front room and each wondered privately why Santa had not placed any presents under the scraggly tree. Mama saw the sense of moral outrage and betrayal in their eyes as they stared at the empty socks lined up along the couch. The children did not say anything aloud, although Buddy's lower lip trembled and Lela's head was bowed down until her chin was nearly on her chest. "Merry Christmas!" Mama told them. "We should sing Christmas carols!"

"The porch! He couldn't get down the stovepipe; the presents are on the porch!" Ginny suddenly realized, and in a mad scramble the girls rushed to the porch, Domio and Bird right behind them. The six returned in disappointed silence to the dining table, and Mama could hardly bear it any longer. She had them put their coats on over their nightgowns and pajamas and follow her out to the back yard. They were mystified at the severe breech in Christmas morning protocol. Frost was heavy in the night and the brown grass glistened under its icy covering. Lela heard the far off train whistle and of course grew excited.

"It's her old train," Ginny groused, her stomach protesting its empty state. "We might as well wave; it's the only thing going on this morning." The rosy dawn was gone and the frosty nip in the air made the gray skies gloomy.

"And I wrote Santa, too," Buddy said dejectedly as she tied and untied knots in her braids, and kicked at a rock.

"Oh, knock it off," Domio told them. "You'd have gotten coal anyway." Buddy stuck out her tongue but did not reply. If her name was on Santa's 'naughty' list after all, it would not help matters to argue on Christmas morning.

The girls did not see two men enter the back yard field through the gate, but Mama did and waved them on in. Domio glanced at her curiously but said nothing. One of the men held a camera and the other held a steno pad and pencil, courtesy of the Lawton newspaper.

Lela pulled her thin winter coat's edges together and held them with one hand as she raised the other hand to wave. The roar of the approaching engine made their hearts race as always, and despite the heavy disappointment in the air the other children caught her enthusiasm to greet the train. To the children's astonishment, instead of racing on its way the locomotive slowed until it came to a stop on the tracks right behind the house. The steam hissed as it escaped, and the whistle sounded louder than ever and made the children jump. Lela's arm stopped moving in mid-air as if frozen as they all stared at the train.

"Is it broken?" Domio asked hesitantly.

Buddy quickly avowed, "I didn't do it."

Malvin waved at Lela from the cab of the engine. Beside him on the steps of the cab stood a round-bellied man with a white beard and a familiar red suit with white trim and matching cap.

"It's Santa Claus!" Lela shrieked, "*He's on my train!*" As she stared in dumbfounded awe, the cameraman took a picture of her.

"Ho, Ho, Ho," Harry chortled as he eased his way down the steps in the unfamiliar overstuffed suit, which until only minutes ago had hung on a hook in the cab. The Watson children scrambled and had him surrounded in seconds. Only Baby Bird remained with Mama. She pointed at the more familiar train instead of the fat man in red and chattered away, her verbosity masked by indecipherable baby language.

Malvin climbed down from the cab and Lela ran to hug him. She was as small and thin as she looked from the train. Dutch and other crewmembers played the part of elves as they brought Santa his "bag of goodies" as well as presents too large to fit into it. Santa/Harry pulled brightly wrapped packages out of the bag and called each child's name as he read it on the gift. Every gift elicited either an excited shriek from a girl, or a wide smile and polite "thank you" from Domio.

"I never saw such a Christmas in my life!" Ginny whooped to Santa.

"I knew you'd come," Buddy said, "but I never knew you'd be takin' a train." Harry let out a laugh and quickly corrected it into a hearty "Ho, ho, ho." Buddy beamed at him. This Santa was the real deal, after all.

Dutch explained, "Well, you know Rudolph and the other reindeer were all worn out from working all night, but since Santa knew you kids wave at the Frisco trains he asked if he could just catch a ride with us." Annie and Ginny gulped and glanced at each other, recalling their irritation and derision at Lela's persistent train waving.

"It's mostly Lela who waves," Annie finally admitted.

"Well, you're all good kids, I can tell," Dutch replied and won a heart-stopping smile from Ginny.

"Yes, but Lela's been good for four whole years," she admitted.

Curious passengers crowded to the windows to watch and some even debarked to watch the proceedings. They had been told the train would make a very special stop and why, but even with that few were prepared for the emotion of the scene. They were in awe at the spirit of giving they were privy to witness. They were also surprised at the children, who despite their obvious lack of means and their overwhelming excitement of the moment, remembered to say "thank you" for every gift.

Lela received her most cherished wish, a Tiny Tears doll complete with fancy covered baby carriage and doll clothes. Malvin briefly explained to Lela that Santa asked his wife to help him find the clothes for the doll so the elves could make presents for the other children. He suddenly regretted it, and hoped it would not spoil the Santa part of the story for the little girl.

"What's your wife's name?" Lela asked.

"My wife? Her name is Eva Belle," Malvin told her.

"Then that's what my baby's name is going to be," Lela said decisively as she cradled the doll lovingly in her arms. "Eva Belle," she crooned.

Malvin had to clear his throat of the sudden lump in it. Eva had taken it upon herself to hand sew every one of the twenty-five articles of clothing for the doll. Every bit of lace and ribbon and tuck and gather represented hours of painstaking work. This little girl had no way to know any of that. The doll would be Eva Belle because it was Malvin the engineer's wife's name, and that was the important thing to Lela. Malvin looked into the crowd of passengers nearby. Eva was there and heard Lela's words. Eva reached for a handkerchief and smiled at Malvin.

As the Watson children giggled in unbridled excitement at the unexpected largess, the photographer continued to take photos. He posed the family with Santa and their gifts with the train in the background as the reporter scribbled in his steno pad rapidly.

The superintendent quietly slipped an envelope to Mama. "The train crew was so successful gathering funds, there's enough money left over for a shopping spree for you and the kids this morning in Lawton." Mama's eyes watered.

"I can't tell you how much this means," she said in a wavering voice.

"I can't tell you how much *this* means," he replied as he took in the scene. It was more than just the publicity the story was sure to generate. The word publicity itself sounded unforgivably crass in light of the joy of innocent faces and the gratitude in a mother's eyes. "Eva will go with you and the rest of the children with the photographer to Lawton, but the crew would like to give Lela a special Christmas ride there in the cab." Mama could only nod; she could not trust herself to speak.

The 'elves' took the presents to the house as 'Santa' told Lela about her special Frisco present. As the little girl was lifted into the engine cab the passengers broke into spontaneous applause. They re-boarded the train, and people who were strangers on the trip to Elgin conversed like old friends over the unexpected bonus the 'Santa Express' provided. The spirit of Christmas ran rampant through every compartment.

Lela never dreamed of such a grand moment as this, and her wide-eyed wonder made the short trip to Lawton all the merrier. She was in the cab of the very train she saw every day, and she was curious about every knob and switch. Malvin answered all her questions, and "Santa" held her up so she could pull the whistle cord. She did so with all the gusto a seven-year-old could give on Christmas morning, and waved out the cab window just as her heroes did.

The train stop was not the end of the adventure as Lela thought it would be. The crew took Lela to her first restaurant visit, where she felt wonderfully grown up. It was just like the movies; waitresses asked what she wanted to eat, the food was brought out in grand style and she did not have to wash the dishes afterwards. She ate the first "store-made" hamburger she ever tasted. They also gave her the first dollar bill she ever owned.

"I'm rich now," she marveled. "A whole dollar!"

Stores were asked weeks ahead of time to open especially for the family for just a little while on

Christmas and they all complied. What was more, none of them accepted a penny from Mama no matter how hard she tried to pay for the purchases with the money from the train. Every store donated all the items the family selected. It was another unexpected but happy turnabout that even the railroad crew did not count on. They encouraged her to use the money on bills and groceries, and that was what she did.

"I kind of hate to get back on the train now," Malvin said, but the volunteer crew that took their places in Lawton would need to be replaced for the return trip so they could enjoy Christmas too. "It was worth it though, wasn't it?"

"It surely was," Harry sighed.

"Dagnabbit," Dutch muttered as he wiped his eyes with a red rag, "I'm as weepy as an ol' willer tree."

The newspaper reporter returned to the newsroom by the time the pictures were developed. Typewriter keys clacked rapidly for the evening edition. His editor whistled at the copy; he knew an above-the-fold, page one Living section story when he saw one. The story was picked up by the wire service and made the evening paper in almost every major market across the country. What editor could resist such a charming story; what reader would not react to such a tale on Christmas night?

In Los Angeles, the newspaper photo of a wide-eyed child gazing in awe at the train that carried Santa Claus to her house so moved actor Lon Chaney Jr., he wrote a letter to the editor to comment on it: "If a picture is worth a thousand words, then the joy and wonder on little Lela's face is worth nothing less."

Another photo caused a stir of concern. Lela's cotton socks were hastily pulled on that morning, and the subsequent running and jumping made one sock slip down past her heel. Lela did not notice her sock had fallen and neither anyone else at the time, but sharp-eyed newspaper readers noticed and wondered if it was a bandage. Perhaps the little girl needed or just had surgery on her foot? Whatever the reason, readers inundated the Lawton newspaper office with worried calls and offers to help pay for her medical expenses.

Mama was astonished when the reporter returned with the news, and she assured him that Lela's foot was just fine. Furthermore, the fresh elastic in the new socks the stores gave them for Christmas would not slip down past her heel in the future.

"Well, people are offering to send you money for medical bills they think you have," the reporter said.

"But we don't need it. The money the railroad gave us bought food and that was the most pressing thing," Mama said cheerfully. "Now that they will have good meals, the children will be healthy as horses. Their father has a good lead on a job now, so we should be fine." There was no guile in her to be found no matter how hard he looked.

But the reporter's cynicism saw plenty of scams over the years and he knew if anything could have guaranteed a big payoff it was a photogenic little girl, a heartwarming Christmas story, and a tear-jerking follow up. "Well," he said carefully to test the waters, "other folks going through tough times might see it as an opportunity."

Mama lifted her chin slightly and said with quiet dignity, "Mr. Watson and I don't approve of stealing. Other folks might do that, but we aren't other folks."

"No, m'am," the reporter said with respect as he rose to his feet, "You sure aren't, and I'm sorry to sound as if you were."

"I'm sure you didn't mean to," Mama said, "but even if we never have another penny to our name, we won't let our kids be dishonest."

"And that," the reporter told the photographer that night over a beer, "will teach me to not be such a cynic. What was I thinking? That little girl went out and waved at that train every single day literally out of the goodness of her heart. I reckon that had to come from somewhere."

Malvin and Santa aboard the Red Ball Express

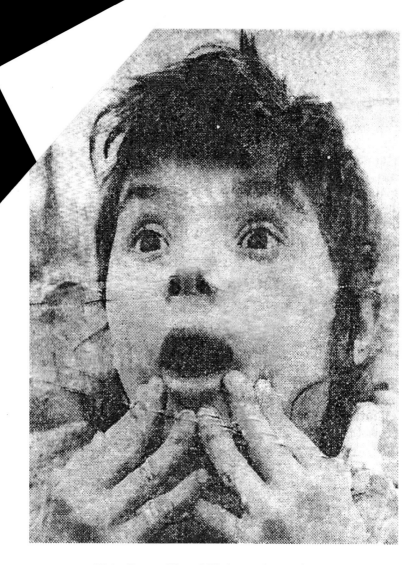

"It's Santa Claus! He's on my train!"

Santa Claus brings Christmas cheer

Mama, Domio, Bird, Annie, Lela, Malvin, Ginny, Santa

and Buddy

The Oklahoma City Times

Jay Michael Jones

(AP)   (UPI)   THIRD & A AVE., LAWTON, OKLAHOMA

MERRY CHRISTMAS—Lela Rae Watson of Elgin smiles happily after receiving a present from Santa Claus who came all the way from the North Pole on the Frisco Meteor. The train made a special stop in front of Lela Rae's house so the present could be delivered. Lela Rae, after a good year of Frisco trainmen, to whom she has been waving for several years. She is seven years old, in the second grade, and has been a good girl. (See picture, Page 2)

Child's Friendly Wave, Smile Wins 'Em
Frisco Meteor's Crew Brings Santa To Door Of Elgin Tots

By TOM SHARROCK
Staff Writer

ELGIN — The Watson kiddies are having a merry Christmas. Especially Lela Rae.

Lela Rae — she's the seven-year-old — arranged for Santa Claus to pay a special visit yesterday afternoon. He didn't come in a sleigh; he came aboard the Frisco Meteor, which made a special stop right in front of the Watson home.

Actually, the Frisco trainmen arranged the stop. They even contacted Santa for Lela Rae, but it was because she is so cute.

You see, Lela Rae, who lives right by the tracks, started waving to them four years ago.

Rain or shine, she was right there. The fence by the tracks has a big gap where she has crawled through to wait for the train.

A couple of months ago one of the trainmen threw her a letter asking what she wanted for Christmas.

She told them.

AND THE METEOR, you know, goes clear up to the North Pole—to St. Louis, at least—so it was no trick at all for the train crew to in a good word for Lela Rae and the other little Watsons.

"Ho, ho, ho," laughed Santa. "I'll even ride the Meteor down if you'll stop long enough for me to deliver her presents in person."

The Lawton newspaper checks in

88

1960 at Bristow – Domio, Annie, Papa, Ginny, Lela,

Buddy and Bird (in front)

Mama

CPSIA information can be obtained at www.ICGtesting.com
Printed in the USA
LVOW100951250613

340107LV00002B/2/P